ARGENTINA

LES AND DAISY FEARNS

Evans

TITLES IN THE COUNTRIES OF THE WORLD SERIES:
ARGENTINA • AUSTRALIA • BRAZIL • CANADA • CHINA
EGYPT • FRANCE • GERMANY • INDIA • ITALY • JAPAN
KENYA • MEXICO • NIGERIA • POLAND • UNITED KINGDOM
USA • VIETNAM

Published by Evans Brothers Limited
2A Portman Mansions
Chiltern Street
London W1U 6NR

VISIT OUR WEBSITE
Evans
www.evansbooks.co.uk

First published 2005
© copyright Evans Brothers 2005

British Library Cataloguing in Publication Data
Fearns, Les and Fearns, Daisy
Argentina. – (Countries of the world)
1.Argentina – Juvenile literature
I.Title
982'.065

ISBN 0 237 52759 6

Editor: Daniel Rogers
Designer: Victoria Webb
Picture researchers: Lynda Lines and Frances Bailey
Map artwork by Peter Bull
Charts and graph artwork by Encompass Graphics Ltd

Produced for Evans Brothers Limited by
Monkey Puzzle Media Limited
Gissing's Farm, Fressingfield
Suffolk IP21 5SH, UK

Picture acknowledgements
All photographs by South American Pictures except:
Alamy 21 (Swerve), 30 bottom (Juncal), 32 bottom (A Parada), 36 top (A Parada); Associated Press 57 bottom (Gustavo Ercole); Corbis 14 bottom (Craig Lovell), 43 (Pitchal Frederic/Sygma), 55 (Sergio Pitamitz); Corbis Digital Stock 10 top, back endpapers; Alec Earnshaw 49 bottom; Eye Ubiquitous/Hutchison 17; Fotozonas 27 (Tomeu Ozonas); Photographers Direct.com (Chris Barton Travel Photography) 10 bottom, 14 top; Reuters 26 top (Osvaldo Marcarian), 31 bottom (Mariana Bazo), 33 (Enrique Marcarian), 42 (Enrique Marcarian), 45 top (Enrique Marcarian), 49 top, 56 (Carlos Barria); Rex Features front cover top (SIPA), 8 (SIPA), 51 (SIPA); Robert Harding Picture Library 41 (R Frerck); Still Pictures (Ron Giling) 11, 24, 25 top, 28, 31 top, 35, 38, 39 top, 45 bottom, 47, 57 top; Still Pictures (Russell Gordon/Das Fotoarchiv) 16, 40; Topham Picturepoint 23 (Stuart Cohen/Image Works).

Endpapers (front): The Obelisco and 9 de Julio Avenue in Buenos Aires – the widest avenue in the world.
Title page: Shoppers in Florida, the main shopping street of Buenos Aires.
Imprint and Contents pages: A mate (tea) plantation in Misiones province.
Endpapers (back): The spectacular Iguazú Falls are 20m higher and half as wide again as the Niagara Falls in North America.

CONTENTS

The Argentine flag consists of two blue bands, representing the daytime sky, and a central white band. The sun with a human face is known as the Sun of May, and is based on the image of Viracocha, the Inca sun god.

INTRODUCING ARGENTINA

Buenos Aires and its surrounding area is home to almost one third of all Argentines.

Argentina is the eighth-largest country in the world and the second-largest in South America, after Brazil. The main language is a form of Spanish, known as Castellano. The land covers an area of 2 million km². A country the size of Spain would easily fit five times into the surface area. This is a country of vibrant contrasts, from subtropical jungles in the north, over high deserts, mountain ranges and wide flat plains, to glaciers in the south.

KEY DATA

Official Name: The Republic of Argentina
Area: 2,766,890km²
Population: 37,740,400 (2001 census)
Official Language: Spanish
Main Cities: Buenos Aires (capital)
                 Córdoba
                 Mendoza
                 La Plata
                 San Miguel de Tucumán
GDP Per Capita: US$10,880*
Currency: Argentine Peso
Exchange Rate: US$1 = 2.98 pesos
                 £1 = 5.60 pesos

*(2002) Calculated on Purchasing Power Parity basis.
Sources: *CIA World Factbook, 2004*; World Bank; UN Human Development Report, 2003

THE SHAPE OF ARGENTINA

Occupying the south-eastern part of South America, Argentina is roughly triangular in shape. Chile, to the west, shares the longest border of 5,150km, following the Andes mountain range. To the north-west lies the landlocked republic of Bolivia. The rivers Pilcomayo, Paraguay and Paraná flow along the northern borders with Paraguay. Brazil and Uruguay are situated to the north-east, with the River Uruguay creating the border. Argentina also considers part of Antarctica (a region between 25° West and 74° West) as its territory. The UK governs the South Atlantic areas of the Falklands (known in Argentina as the Islas Malvinas), South Georgia and the South Sandwich Islands, but they are claimed by Argentina. The South Atlantic Ocean borders the eastern coast, stretching for almost 5,000km.

PROVINCES OF ARGENTINA

A gaucho on the Pampas – the traditional Argentine cowboy.

A DIVERSE COUNTRY

Argentina's diversity is most clearly seen in its varied landscapes, which include the Andes mountain range, the extensive, flat, fertile plains of central Argentina and Patagonia, and Tierra del Fuego in the south. Argentina is home to a wide range of wildlife and, because of its differing environments, it also supports a varied array of vegetation.

About 90 per cent of the population live in urban areas. The capital city, Buenos Aires, is home to both rich and poor alike and, with a population of 12 million inhabitants, is the third-largest city in the world.

Argentina is rich in natural resources and has a well-established agricultural industry. The tourist industry is developing quickly to take advantage of the interest in adventure and activity holidays.

Argentina is a rich mix of cultures, combining the traditions of South America with the influences brought by European immigrants in a land of great variety and promise.

THE COLLAPSE OF 2002

In 2002, after some years of prosperity, the Argentine economy collapsed (see page 44). Factories closed down and millions of people lost their jobs. Most people lost all their savings as the national currency, the peso, became less valuable. At one stage, over 40 per cent of the population lived in poverty. Argentina's international debts were bigger than those of any other country in history. There were five presidents in three years.

Since 2002, Argentina has recovered fast but the impact of the collapse has influenced the country considerably.

LANDSCAPE AND CLIMATE

Iguazú Falls on the Alto Paraná river on the border with Brazil and Paraguay.

ARGENTINA'S LANDSCAPES

Argentina contains a huge variety of landscapes, from the high mountains of the Andes in the west to the flat grasslands of the Pampas in the east, and the fertile subtropical north-east to the vast Patagonian plateau in the south.

THE NORTH AND THE CHACO

The northern regions of Argentina differ greatly and can be divided into three sections – montane, savannah and subtropical. The north-west is mountainous, consisting of layers of sedimentary rocks, including limestone, sandstone, marl and clay, containing fossils. The Chaco is an extensive, flat plain with a mixture of savannah grassland, marsh, thorn scrub and caranday palms. Slow-flowing, meandering rivers cross this area and drain into the Río Paraná.

The rolling countryside in the north-east is covered with subtropical vegetation, which grows abundantly on the rich soils and in the warm, moist conditions. This area has two major rivers, the Paraná and the Uruguay. The magnificent Iguazú Falls are situated on the Alto Paraná river.

A herd of llamas on the grasslands of the high plains in Jujuy province.

naturally, but eucalyptus trees have been introduced by landowners to provide shade and shelter, and are now a common sight near small towns and settlements. Crossing the Pampas is a network of busy roads. Long-distance buses run regular, efficient services despite the huge distances.

ESTANCIAS

The unique environment of the Pampas has given rise to a kind of settlement called an estancia. Built by the original Spanish settlers, these were first set up around Buenos Aires as centres of cattle herding. The first estancias were large enough to support 900 cattle – about 2,000 hectares. Some are now over 10,000 hectares. The estancias were so isolated that often a school or a church was built for the family and the workers, as well as housing and farm buildings.

Today, many estancias combine the traditional business of rearing animals or growing crops with tourism.

Horses are still the main way of working and exploring the estancia.

THE PAMPAS

This is a vast, fertile, flat plain stretching for hundreds of kilometres, fanning out from Buenos Aires to the west and south. The soils are fine, wind-blown loess on which cereals, pulses and grass flourish. Estancias, the Argentine name for cattle ranches, are found here. Cattle are raised for beef and dairy production, especially in the province of Buenos Aires, where higher rainfall produces lusher grass. There are few rivers in this region, with the exception of the Río Salado. Water for domestic and agricultural use has to be pumped up to the surface by means of wind pumps. Hardly any trees grow here

THE ANDES

Running the length of Argentina's western border with Chile is the spectacular Andes mountain range. The rugged, snow-capped peaks rise to over 3,000m and the stark terrain is constantly being eroded and reshaped by ice, water, extremes of temperature and wind. Earthquakes occur regularly in the surrounding areas, especially in Mendoza province. The Lake District is located in Neuquén province, where a string of glacial lakes have formed in deep, wooded valleys behind dams of glacial moraine, left after the end of the last ice age. Much of this picturesque area is now designated as a national park, offering a wide variety of adventure and outdoor activity pursuits. There are seven crossing points along the Andes between Argentina and Chile, which remain open all year round, weather permitting.

PATAGONIA AND ANTARCTICA

Much of southern Argentina is part of a region called Patagonia (which also includes southern Chile). This is a huge, treeless plateau, sloping gently from the foothills of the Andes towards the east coast. The Valdes Peninsula contains the country's lowest point of land, at 40m below sea level. One of the world's few advancing glaciers, the Moreno Glacier, is in the Glacier National Park. Here the Andes Mountains are generally lower and there are two extensive ice fields. The most southerly city in the world, Ushuaia, is on the north shore of the Beagle Channel in Tierra del Fuego. Many of the ships carrying scientists and tourists to Antarctica leave from the harbour in Ushuaia. In 1943 Argentina made a territorial claim on an area of the Antarctic and it now has six scientific stations there.

CASE STUDY
ACONCAGUA

The south face of Mount Aconcagua, the highest peak in the southern hemisphere.

Aconcagua is a Quechuan word meaning 'stone sentinel'. At 6,960m, it is the highest peak in the southern hemisphere. This now extinct volcano last erupted millions of years ago, but has been raised to its current altitude by tectonic forces. The volcano is surrounded by many other high peaks, such as Mount Cuerno (at 5,450m) and Mount Catedral (5,200m). All lie within the Aconcagua Provincial Park.

Mountaineers from all over the world travel to Argentina to climb peaks such as Aconcagua. It was first climbed in 1897, by the Swiss mountain guide Matthias Zurbriggen. His route, known as the Ruta Normal, is still the most frequently used. The extreme altitude, severe winds, and cold temperatures make an ascent very challenging. In 1934, a second route was pioneered by a Polish team along a route known today as the Polish Glacier.

Lago Nahuel Huapi in the Lake District, Neuquén province.

This glacier is over 30km long, 5km wide and, at its snout, has a wall of moving ice over 60m high. Visitors watch and listen as pieces of ice break off the front of the glacier and plunge into the river. The glacier is best seen from a series of walkways on the opposite side of the Brazo Rico river, or by taking a walking tour both on and under the ice. Several times the glacier has advanced so rapidly that it blocked the river channel, causing flooding in the local area. However, in recent years the rate of glacial movement has slowed, raising worries that global warming is changing the local climate.

Visitors get a spectacular view of the Moreno Glacier in the Glacier National Park, Patagonia.

Storm clouds gather in the north over the plains of Jujuy province.

CLIMATE

Being in the southern hemisphere, Argentina's seasons are opposite to those in the northern hemisphere. Winter is from June to August and summer from November to January. Stretching for a distance of around 3,500km from 22° South to 55° South, and from the Atlantic coast in the east to the high Andes in the west, the country has four main climatic regions.

THE PAMPAS

This region generally has rainfall of between 500mm and 1,000mm a year although droughts and floods do occur. Winters are mild, with temperatures of 5°C to 10°C, and summers are warm, between 25°C and 35°C. More rainfall occurs during the summer than in winter, and electrical thunderstorms, or *tormentas*, occur all year round. The eastern and northern areas are generally the wettest and most humid. Strong westerly winds, called the Pampero, are hot and dry and can cause dusty conditions.

THE NORTH AND THE CHACO

Temperatures remain quite high all year round, between 15°C and 39°C. The combination of heat and humidity may be uncomfortable in the summer months, as this is the cloudier, wetter season. Each month, over 75mm of rain falls throughout the year and flooding is common. Misiones province in the far north-east is subtropical, and for much of the time conditions are sunny and dry. Occasional cold spells in winter may reduce temperatures but generally it is mild or warm.

WESTERN ARGENTINA

Lying in the rain shadow of the Andes, the annual rainfall here is below 250mm and is very unreliable. Droughts are frequent and

CASE STUDY
SAN CARLOS DE BARILOCHE

Swiss-style architecture in the tourist resort of San Carlos de Bariloche.

The town of San Carlos de Bariloche is situated on the shores of Lago Nahuel Huapi in Argentina's Lake District. It is surrounded by snow-capped peaks. Founded in 1903 it became famous for its chocolate industry, set up by Swiss immigrants. The town's architecture also reflects this ancestry, as many buildings are 'Alpine' in style.

San Carlos de Bariloche is a major tourist destination, where summer visitors can walk, cycle, climb or fish. Horse-riding, water sports and bird-watching activities are also popular. On the surrounding lakes, ferries carry day trippers on pleasure cruises or take passengers to the borders of Chile.

In winter, San Carlos de Bariloche is Argentina's major ski resort, with 5,000 hectares of groomed slopes, over 64km of ski trails and 34 ski lifts catering for 20,000 skiers.

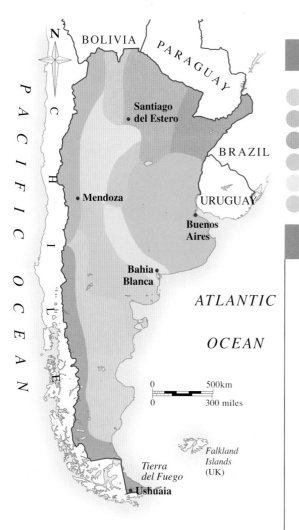

CLIMATE ZONES

- Tropical highland
- Subtropical, with dry season
- Subtropical, no dry season
- Temperate wet
- Temperate semi arid
- Temperate highland
- Dry upland
- Semi arid
- Dry Patagonian
- Arid Andean
- Wet Andean

TEMPERATURE AND RAINFALL

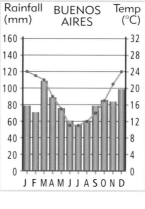

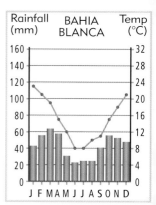

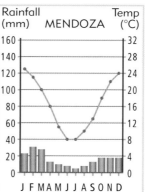

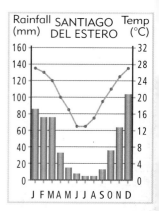

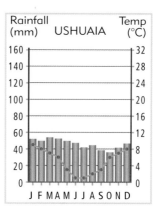

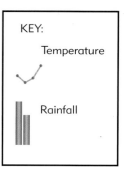

KEY:

Temperature

Rainfall

often prolonged. Most rain falls during summer, which is generally hot and very sunny. Temperatures vary according to altitude, from well below freezing in the mountains to over 30°C in summer in lowland areas.

PATAGONIA

This enormous region is dry, with average annual rainfall of only 130mm. In the north, winter temperatures range between 5°C and 10°C, rising in the summer to between 12°C and 25°C. The warm Zonda winds blow across northern Patagonia from the west. Further south, winters are long, dark and very cold, with temperatures near or below freezing. Summer conditions rarely see temperatures above 15°C.

NATURAL RESOURCES

Taking samples at El Aguilar, Jujuy province, the highest mine in Argentina. It produces lead, silver and zinc.

Argentina takes its name from *argentum*, the Latin word for silver. The Spanish conquistadores who invaded the country exploited the silver deposits in the seventeenth and eighteenth centuries, sending most of this precious metal back to Europe. Today other resources provide the country with its wealth. Mineral deposits, rich agricultural land, forests and an abundance of wildlife and areas of natural beauty are all part of the natural resources of this vast land.

MINERALS

Although deposits of coal, iron ore, tin, lead, zinc, tungsten, mica and borax are on a small scale, recent investment from international companies has expanded the precious metals industry, especially gold, in Patagonia.

Natural gas and oil reserves are located in the north-west, in the region of Cuyo in the west, in Neuquén, in the far south of Patagonia and in the Golfo San Jorge. Proven oil reserves stand at 2.9 billion barrels. Argentina is one of the few countries in South America that exports oil and oil products, which it sells to countries nearby, such as Chile, Bolivia and Paraguay. The economic and political crisis in 2002 affected the oil industry, though it is better off than other industries due to the high international demand for oil.

ENERGY

Today Argentina generates 49 per cent of its electricity in power plants that use the country's abundant supply of natural gas. Gas is also used as a domestic fuel by the majority of the population, although many homes are not supplied by pipeline and have to rely on LPG (liquefied petroleum gas). About 14 per cent (1.1 million) of all vehicles are powered by CNG, compressed natural gas, and the numbers are increasing every year.

Large dams on the Limay, Paraná and Uruguay rivers produce HEP (hydroelectric power) to generate 42 per cent of the total electricity output. Coal, oil, charcoal and wood account for a further 3 per cent of electricity production. Wind power is used but adds less than 0.2 per cent to total generation.

Coal
Oil and gas
Ferrous metals
Rare metals
Radioactive metals
Non-ferrous metals

≋≋ Major HEP schemes
•••• Major oil/gas pipelines

ELECTRICITY GENERATION (2003)

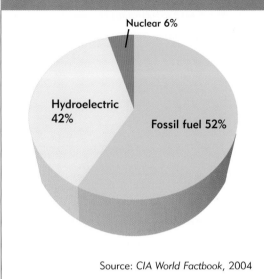

Nuclear 6%

Hydroelectric 42%

Fossil fuel 52%

Source: *CIA World Factbook*, 2004

In 2002, Argentina was the fourth-largest oil producer in Latin America at 812,000 barrels per day. All production is now by foreign-owned companies. Just under 50 per cent of the oil is exported, mainly through pipelines to neighbouring countries.

CASE STUDY
YPF – YACIMIENTOS PETROLIFEROS FISCALES

A YPF oil refinery in the south of Patagonia near Comodoro Rivadavia.

In 1897, the first major oil reserves were discovered near Comodoro Rivadavia in Patagonia, on the Atlantic coast 2,000km south of Buenos Aires. In 1922, the government created the first national oil company, YPF, which became responsible for all major oil exploration and extraction activities. Further oil deposits were discovered in the provinces of Neuquén and Mendoza. For 70 years, YPF enjoyed a near monopoly of oil extraction and production, but deregulation of the industry in the 1990s created competition and took the company out of government ownership. Today, 99 per cent of YPF is owned by the Spanish oil company Repsol.

Oil production has developed and expanded, with over 300 million barrels of crude oil being produced in 2001. YPF refines and processes oil in large petrochemical plants in Luján de Cuyo, near Mendoza, and Plaza Huincul near Neuquén.

Mixed farming is common on the Pampas. Almost half the wheat grown is used to feed cattle.

MEAT AND GRAINS

The rich soils of the Pampas, which cover much of central Argentina, are ideal for growing crops and grass for cattle.

Argentina has long been a world leader in the export of raw meat. In 2003, it was the fifth-largest beef-producing country in the world, producing 4.8 per cent of the world supply. Cooked and canned meats are also important exports.

The Pampas is known as the bread basket of Argentina. In 2003, 15 million tonnes of wheat were produced there, and a similar amount of maize was grown. Although much of this is

A gaucho herding cattle in Entre Ríos.

CORNED BEEF

Before the introduction of large-scale refrigeration or freezers, beef was preserved by salting or pickling. Pampas cattle were driven in huge herds to river ports, from where ships transported cargoes of salted beef carcasses, hides or tinned beef. In the 1880s, the Benitez brothers started a small beef-salting business at Fábrica Colón on the banks of the Uruguay River. The meat was cooked with large amounts of salt and then canned. The term 'corned' beef comes from the word 'corns', used to describe the granular salt pieces that were used, and has nothing to do with the cereal or what the cows were fed.

The business grew and, by 1905, it had been sold to a German engineer. Named Puerto Liebig, the company flourished, producing tinned corned beef, beef extract and canned tongue meat until 1980. It also marketed the world-famous brand of corned beef – Fray Bentos. The factory at Fray Bentos is on the opposite bank of the river in Uruguay, but it too processed thousands of tons of beef. Argentine corned beef is still sold in shops around the world.

used to feed the 54 million cattle and 17 million sheep, more than half is exported. Argentina has a commercial advantage in that crops are harvested at seasons opposite to those of the northern hemisphere, and so it has few seasonal competitors.

THE WINE INDUSTRY

Spanish vines were first introduced in the 1550s by Jesuit missionaries, who settled in the Andes foothills. The industry was small scale and local until, in 1885, a group of Europeans opened a railway link between Buenos Aires and Mendoza. This gave the vineyards access to a larger market for their wine in the capital. Until the 1990s, most wine was produced for the domestic market, mainly from a single grape variety.

The wine-producing regions extend for over 2,000km along the western side of the country, from Cafayate in the far north down to the low-lying areas of the Río Negro valley in Patagonia.

Wine production has developed rapidly for two reasons: vast foreign investment of money and modern technology, and as a result of the economic crisis in 2002, when Argentine wines became very affordable for international markets. Argentina is now recognised as a major New World wine producer, and is the fifth-largest wine producer in the world.

CASE STUDY
WINE GROWING IN MENDOZA

Situated at a similar (but southern) latitude to the French, Italian and Californian vineyards, the climate and terrain of Mendoza are ideal for all the major varieties of grape. Rainfall is less than 200mm a year but abundant snow from the nearby Andes mountains allows irrigation from the rivers of melted snow. The main grape varieties grown in this area are Malbec, Cabernet Sauvignon, Syrah and Chardonnay.

Around 70 per cent of all Argentine wine is produced here – 1.5 million tonnes annually out of a total Argentine production of 2.2 million tonnes. Picking is still mainly done by hand, but wine production is now highly industrialised following massive foreign investment. Mendoza wine is the most commonly

Grapes being picked in a Mendoza vineyard during the harvest in late February.

exported Argentine wine. The main export markets for its quality wine are the UK, the USA and Brazil. Lower quality table wines are exported mainly to South Africa, Russia and Paraguay. Most bodegas (wineries) are still owned by Argentines, though French, British, Spanish and Chilean companies have invested heavily in order to control the quality of the wines that are exported.

Young and mature eucalyptus being grown in a plantation close to the River Uruguay.

FORESTRY

Situated mainly in mountain areas, away from centres of population, Argentina's 34.6 million hectares of forest are relatively unused. The most-harvested trees are elm and willow, for cellulose production; white quebracho, for fuel; red quebracho, for tannin (used for tanning leather); and cedar, for the manufacture of furniture. Other economically important trees are oak, araucaria, pine, eucalyptus, and cypress. Thanks to foreign investment, timber production has increased since the mid-1990s. The largest growth has been in the production of wood pulp for the paper and cardboard industries. New plantations of sustainable softwood trees, mostly pine and eucalyptus, are being established, especially in northern Argentina, where the climate produces rapid growth. There are worries that these plantations are destroying natural grassland habitats for wildlife. Birds such as long-tailed tyrants and spinetails are now less common than ten years ago.

SPORT FISHING

Fresh-water and sea fishing are very popular in Argentina, both for local people and, in recent years, for tourists. In almost every part of the country, a wide variety of fishing sites is available in lakes, ponds, dam reservoirs and mountain streams.

Sea fishing along the 3,500km Atlantic Ocean coasts offers catches such as black-mouth and fair croaker, herring smelt and pomfret. Deep-sea sport fishing is a growing tourist activity, with species such as bluenose warehou, Argentine seabass, sea salmon, forkbeard, patagonic mullet and sharks (which can weigh more than 100kg) being caught.

FISHERIES

Although Argentina has a coastline of nearly 5,000km, the fishing industry is comparatively small and mainly located in Mar del Plata, 400km south of Buenos Aires.

Unlike in agriculture, where large estancias and (increasingly international) agribusiness concerns dominate, the fishing industry is mainly based on local cooperatives, often of

Offshore fishing boats at the port of Mar del Plata. These and the larger deep-sea trawlers catch mainly hake, mackerel and hoki.

small vessels. Over 90 per cent of the catch is exported to other South American countries. An extensive salmon and trout farming industry is also developing, with the main markets in Spain, Brazil and the USA.

Rivers such as the Paraná, Uruguay, Salado, de la Plata, and Negro all have plentiful supplies of freshwater fish, including the dorado, tararira, surubí and manguruyú. During August, the Dorado National Celebration takes place in Corrientes, which celebrates the catching of three species of fish: the dorado, the pacu and the surubía catfish. It is Argentina's most important sporting event with an international reputation. Argentina's famed brown trout fishing waters are located in Tierra del Fuego.

Sport fishing in the Nahuel Huapi National Park attracts anglers from all over the world.

THE PEOPLE OF ARGENTINA

Quechua people selling panpipes and *quenas* (flutes) at a market in Humahuaca, Jujuy province.

THE INDIGENOUS POPULATION

Argentina does not have a large number of indigenous people. Unlike other Latin American countries, the majority of Argentines are the descendants of Europeans. Only about 8 per cent are indigenous or *mestizo* (mixed race).

Nowadays there are 13 different native minorities, numbering just over 500,000 people in total. They are found mainly in the poorer northern provinces of Chaco and Jujuy. The largest single group is the Colla, who speak Quechua and who have many links with native groups in Bolivia.

Further south, in Patagonia, the indigenous tribes have nearly vanished. One tribe, the Tehuelches, lives on a reservation and numbers less than 100 people.

THE SPANISH

The first Europeans to arrive were from Spain. The Río de la Plata was first explored in 1517 by a Spanish expedition looking for an Atlantic route to the treasures of Peru. The Spanish also entered the country from Bolivia and Paraguay and settled in the north.

CASE STUDY
THE GAUCHO

Gauchos are the cowboys of the Pampas. They are still a common sight today, although they are just as likely to be seen driving cab trucks as on horseback.

Dressed in traditional baggy, knee-length trousers, beret, handkerchief round the neck, spurs and a sharp knife hanging from his belt, a gaucho is seen very much as part of the tradition of Argentina. The Gauchos are highly respected for their skills in horseriding and with the *boleadoras* (three stones tied together with a rope), which is used to lasso cattle.

Argentines enjoy eating beef, especially in traditional *asado* barbecues or on *parrilla* grills. Argentina has the highest annual beef consumption in the world, about 60kg per person. In Patagonia, where sheep are grazed, mutton replaces beef on the *asado*.

Apart from *asados* or *parrillas*, beef is also eaten in *empanadas*, small pastry snacks with a meat filling. As immigrants arrived from Europe the meat was served up in new ways. For example, *Milanesa*, Italian breaded veal, is also popular. Being a vegetarian in Argentina is a difficult and lonely choice!

An estancia gaucho prepares beef on a *parrilla* for a local celebration.

The most organised of these early northern settlements were those of the Catholic Jesuits. They set up missions where local Indians were protected from the slave trade, taught Christianity and trained to grow crops. They also had to give up their nomadic way of life.

Small numbers of Spanish also began to settle and develop the southern Pampas around Buenos Aires. These grasslands provided excellent grazing for cattle, and the Spanish landowners set up large estates, or estancias, for their herds.

POPULATION STRUCTURE OF ARGENTINA BY RACE

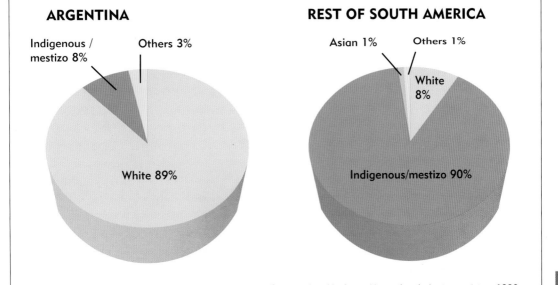

ARGENTINA

Indigenous / mestizo 8%

Others 3%

White 89%

REST OF SOUTH AMERICA

Asian 1%

Others 1%

White 8%

Indigenous/mestizo 90%

Source: *Los Medios y Mercados de Latinoamérica, 1998*

EUROPEAN IMMIGRATION

Most Argentines today are the descendants of European immigrants who came to the country in the nineteenth and early twentieth centuries. Around 1900, Argentina was the sixth most prosperous country in the world and competed with the USA as the main destination for emigrants from Europe. The attractions were many: the wide-open spaces of the interior; work on the new railways that criss-crossed the agricultural Pampas; and employment in the cattle industries of the countryside, towns and cities. More than 250,000 people entered the country each year in a process that continued for another 30 years. Most were from Italy, but Swiss and German immigrants also proved successful farmers in the north. Basque, Irish and Welsh communities grew up, especially in the sheep-herding areas of Patagonia.

IMMIGRANTS IN BUENOS AIRES

Most immigrants arrived on the docks of Buenos Aires and stayed in the city. Today, the results of this immigrant mix can be seen everywhere. There are Italian restaurants, German-language newspapers and Scottish country-dancing clubs. Streets in the centre resemble Paris or Madrid, while the railway stations could be in the UK. Football, introduced by the British and the Italians, is a national passion. There are English, German, French and Italian bilingual schools where pupils are taught not only in their native Spanish but also in the language of their immigrant great grandparents, and Scottish kilts are a common school uniform for girls.

After World War I more immigrants arrived, this time from south-eastern Europe and the Middle East, particularly Armenia, Syria and Lebanon.

CASE STUDY
GAIMAN

One of the several Welsh tea shops in Gaiman, Chubut province.

Gaiman is a small town in Chubut in southern Argentina. A look in the phone book reveals Welsh names, such as Davies, Jones and Williams. Local buildings include Ysgol y Camwy (school), Capel Bethel (chapel), and Tavarn Las (pub).

In the 1860s groups of Welsh people crossed the Atlantic and settled in Argentina. Life was hard: in particular, fresh water was limited. Despite this, many survived and stayed on to build a new life in the country. There are about 20,000 descendants of the Welsh in Chubut today, 6,000 of them in Gaiman, the 'most-Welsh' settlement in the region.

Like the other immigrant groups to the country, successive generations have remembered their roots. Although proudly Argentine, a quarter still speak Welsh alongside Castellano. At present about 700 people – both old and young – are learning Welsh as part of a government scheme to

promote the language in Argentina. The design of many local buildings is taken straight from originals in the mining valleys of South Wales.

The area is beginning to take advantage of its origins. A developing tourist industry is presenting the towns of Gaiman and its neighbours, Trelew and Puerto Madryn, as distinctively Welsh. Tours visit the towns and a popular activity is to go to Gaiman for a cream tea served by an Argentine wearing Welsh national dress!

ABOVE: Once a poor immigrant area of Buenos Aires, these colourful streets in La Boca are now a major tourist attraction.

BELOW: Argentine and international newspapers are easily available at news-stands in Buenos Aires and other main cities.

Overseas immigration still continues. From 1965 to 1985, about 50,000 South Koreans emigrated to Argentina. South Koreans operate about 1,000 businesses in and around Buenos Aires and there are about 300 Korean cultural, athletic and business associations.

A sign of this recent immigrant past is that many Argentines have two passports – an Argentine passport and a passport from their families' country of origin in Europe.

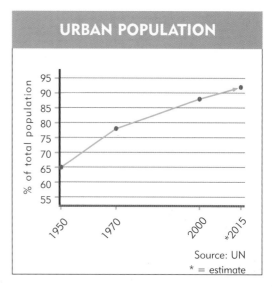

URBAN POPULATION

% of total population

95
90
85
80
75
70
65
60
55

1950 · 1970 · 2000 · *2015

Source: UN
* = estimate

LATIN AMERICAN IMMIGRATION

Although the Argentine economy has many problems today, the country is still far richer than many of its neighbours. This relative prosperity has brought another wave of immigrants, this time from Latin America. Many are indigenous natives of neighbouring Bolivia, Paraguay and Peru who have come to look for work. Until the economic collapse of 2002, it was possible to work as a domestic maid and be able to send US$500 a month (a large amount of money in the Andean countries) home to a family outside Argentina.

Many immigrants are illegal visitors, and an estimated 200,000 undocumented migrants from Bolivia, Paraguay and Peru live and work in Argentina. Most of them are in Buenos Aires. Migrants from the poorer northern and western areas of Argentina have added to the numbers. If they succeed in finding work, it is often low-paid, manual work in service and construction jobs. Many women work as maids in people's houses

ABOVE: Immigrants waiting outside the Bolivian consulate in Buenos Aires to begin the process of getting permission to stay and work legally in Argentina.

Many migrants live in shanty towns, known as *villas*, in and around Buenos Aires. Living conditions there are not easy, and few *villas* have utilities such as water, sewerage and electricity. Like the Europeans who came earlier, the new immigrants hope to find a good job, settle with their family and leave the *villa*. However, it is hard for them to gain the opportunity and education that will equip them for the better paid jobs of the modern economy.

The recent economic downturn has not been kind to these immigrants. They were the first to lose their jobs and their illegal status led to many being deported back to Bolivia, Peru and Paraguay.

EMIGRATION FROM ARGENTINA

Because of recent economic problems, many Argentines have been using their second passports to emigrate and look for work overseas. According to a 2002 survey, one third of the population would leave the

A Paraguayan immigrant dressed in her typical maid's uniform in a house in the wealthy Palermo district of the capital.

country if they could. Between 2000 and 2003, over 250,000 did leave for Europe, mainly the well trained, educated and young. About 10 million of the 37.7 million Argentines are at least half Italian, and Italy allows them to claim Italian citizenship and live in Italy. Many others have the right to emigrate and work in countries such as Spain or Israel.

Although close to the prosperous heart of Buenos Aires, Villa Miserias 31 is the biggest shanty township in the country. It is close to the Retiro coach station where many families arrive from the provinces and nearby countries.

ORIGIN OF IMMIGRANTS TO ARGENTINA, 1857–1940

NATIONALITY	IMMIGRANTS
Italian	2,970,000
Spanish	2,080,000
Eastern Europe	516,000
French	239,000
German and Swiss	196,000
Middle East	174,000
British	75,000
Other	138,000

Source: based on figures in *South American Immigration: Argentina* by Wanda Velez

POPULATION GROWTH

Immigration has been responsible for most of Argentina's population growth since the nineteenth century but, even after the period of mass immigration ended, the population continued to grow. It more than doubled from 17.2 million in 1950 to 37.7 million in 2001.

Although the birth rate is now falling, and is among the lowest in South America, it has been high in the past. Even at its current level of 18 births per 1,000 people, it is still almost 80 per cent higher than the rate in the UK. Large families are common. Argentina also has a well-developed healthcare system, and life expectancy has increased steadily. At 74 years, it is higher than its neighbours.

As a result, Argentina has a healthy population structure – enough people of

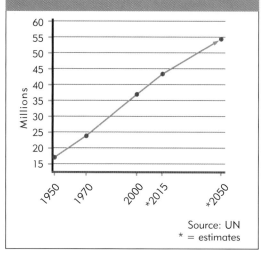

POPULATION 1950–2050

Source: UN
* = estimates

working age to support the growing numbers of the elderly, but without the population explosion of other developing countries.

The container port and skyline of Buenos Aires.

With a population of approximately 12 million people, Buenos Aires is the largest city in Argentina and the largest in South America. As well as the capital city, it is the financial, industrial, commercial, and social centre of Argentina. It has one of the busiest ports in the world, which links to an inland river system connecting the capital to the majority of Argentina as well as to Brazil, Uruguay and Paraguay. The people of Buenos Aires are known as *porteños* (people of the port).

Being so close to the agricultural Pampas, meat, dairy, grain, tobacco, wool and hide products are all processed or manufactured in Buenos Aires. Other leading industries include automobile manufacturing, oil refining, metalworking, machine building, and the production of textiles, chemicals, paper, clothing and beverages.

No other Argentine city approaches the size of Buenos Aires, and no other province has its population or prosperity. Córdoba, the second-largest city, has a population of 1,160,000, the river port of Rosario has 1,157,372 and La Plata, the next-largest, 700,000.

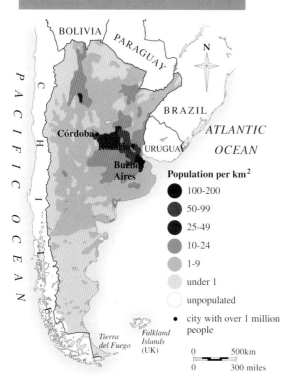

The empty, open Patagonian landscape near Lago Argentino in Santa Cruz province.

POPULATION DISTRIBUTION

In recent years, there has also been acceleration in the growth of urban areas as people move from the countryside to the towns. In 1985, 85 per cent of the population lived in urban centres (25.6 million); by 2000 this had risen to 88 per cent (33 million). Most recent new urban development has been in Patagonia and the north-west. Buenos Aires has continued to be the biggest magnet for the moving population, and more than one third of Argentina's population lives in or around Buenos Aires. There has been a relative decrease in the population of the north-east, the Cuyo area and the Pampas region.

In Greater Buenos Aires the population density is 60 people per km², but most of the country remains very empty and unpopulated, except for the occasional settlement or isolated estancia. Chaco in the north has a population density of 8 people per km². In the south, the vast Patagonian provinces of Santa Cruz, at 1.5 people per km², and Chubut, at 0.6 per km², have far less. Vast open spaces meet the eye in most of Patagonia.

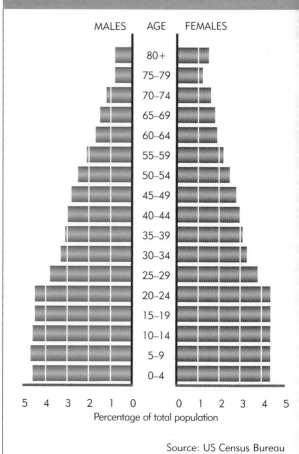

Source: US Census Bureau

EVERYDAY LIFE

A waiter takes an order at the Café La Biela, in fashionable Recoleta, Buenos Aires.

Just as Argentina has many different climates and natural environments, so it also has many different lifestyles. Quality of life is largely dependent on whether you live in the countryside or in the capital, as well as your social position and wealth.

CASE STUDY
THE BUENOS AIRES SUBURB

San Isidro is a suburb of northern Buenos Aires. Most houses are set in their own large grounds and their owners employ maids. Swimming pools are common. Modern shopping malls, such as Unicenter, sell the latest designer products from all over the world. Many children attend private schools. The area has sailing clubs, an international golf course and a racecourse, and car showrooms sell imported luxury cars. There are also expensive restaurants and cafés. Commuters travel in new, air-conditioned electric trains into the city, where they might work as managers, accountants or lawyers.

Buenos Aires has many prosperous suburbs where people live comfortably and enjoy a good standard of living. It also has many *villas*. Some *villas* have only a handful of families, others have several thousand. The inhabitants are mostly left on their own to build and provide their own basic facilities. As unemployment in the *villas* is high and incomes low, this is very difficult to achieve. *Villas* are likely to be bulldozed at short notice to make way for new development.

Outside the capital and big cities is another Argentina, in which small agricultural towns and settlements are dotted along the main roads.

A view of the lush Buenos Aires suburb of San Isidro where many prosperous families live, close to the Río de la Plata.

In most of Argentina, outside the cities, settlements are small and spread out, and daily life is centred on the land.

San Antonio de Areco is a typical country town on the Pampas, with traditional, Spanish-colonial-style leafy streets set out in grids around central squares. Farmhands in gaucho dress can be seen riding around the town on horseback or driving their trucks. Industry is workshop based and uses the raw materials of the land: for example, leather is worked into saddles, belts and bags. There was a railway line connecting San Antonio to Buenos Aires. It is now closed down and buses travel the route instead.

Modern Argentina can be best seen in the showrooms that display tractors and other farming equipment. Large grain silos can be seen outside the town. This is an agricultural community and big commercial farms still provide most employment.

The main square of San Antonio de Areco, built on the site of the first cattle corral in the area.

A few blocks from the centre of San Isidro is another Argentina: the Argentina of the *villa*, or shanty. Across the country, thousands of the poorest people live in *villas*. Some buildings are made of wood or brick, others from recycled materials. Walls can be made from metal sheets or advertising hoardings. Few *villas* have services like clean water, sewerage or electricity, and health conditions are far below the national average. Infant mortality is nearly three times the national average, at 52 deaths per 1,000 births. Violence and crime are common and many *villas* are no-go areas for the police. Some of the *villa* children are educated in local state schools; others, especially those of illegal immigrant families, receive no education at all unless the *villa* can set up a small class of its own. Without a proper education, it is hard for someone to get a good job that will take them out of the *villa*.

Villa dwellers work hard to improve their conditions. Although some help is provided by charities, self-help is the main source of improvement. Funds are raised by community events to try to get basic utilities for the *villa*. More recently, *villas* have begun to organise themselves nationally in order to seek government help.

Families in the *villa* use whatever materials they can find to build their homes.

31

A computer class in a private school in Buenos Aires

EDUCATION

Argentina has a well-educated and highly qualified population and a literacy rate of 97 per cent – one of the highest in Latin America; the figure for the UK is 99 per cent.

However, education is under pressure. More Argentines receive a secondary education than any of their neighbours, but 20 per cent do not attend secondary school. The government has introduced reforms but lack of money means there are not enough teachers or books in many state schools. Between 1990 and 1999, Brazil spent an average of 4.7 per cent of its GDP (gross domestic product) on education, and Bolivia 4.8 per cent; Argentina allocated only 3.2 per cent.

For those who can afford it, private education is expanding. About one in five primary pupils attend private schools, most going on to private secondary schools. The Government has allowed private universities to be set up, which has increased the number of graduates. Today, 48 per cent of 18- to 23-year-olds in Argentina take part in higher education. This compares favourably with 37 per cent in Chile and 16.5 per cent in Brazil.

A primary school class in Córdoba. State school pupils wear a white coat for a uniform.

(In the UK, 59 per cent attend higher education.) However, many of the graduates cannot find suitable work and, in recent years, more and more of them have been leaving to work in Europe or the USA.

SOCIAL WELFARE

For over 50 years, Argentina has provided basic healthcare for all. Between 1945 and 1953, a welfare state was created which still exists today, and national insurance is used to provide medical care for the poorest people. Laws give women many maternity benefits, and a pension scheme helps the elderly. Argentina also provides a comprehensive, subsidised programme of treatment for AIDS sufferers. In 30 years, infant mortality has fallen from 71 deaths in every 1,000 births (1970) to just 19 (2002), and life expectancy has risen from 67 to 74 years. Argentina now has one of Latin America's highest doctor-to-population ratios (30.5 doctors per 10,000 people). This compares favourably with the USA (29 doctors per 10,000) and the UK (18 per 10,000).

The recent economic collapse has put pressure on health spending. In the late 1990s, annual health expenditure grew by 9.5 per cent only to decrease by 9 per cent in 2001. In 2004, US$180 was spent on every

Weighing a child at the Faimalla hospital in northern Tucumán province.

Argentine compared with US$650 in 1999. Health resources are severely stretched and hospitals report shortages of basic supplies. The costs of funding the state system, and of buying imported medicines with a devalued currency, are rising. The quality of the treatment available is falling. Benefits such as pensions are also being reduced. Just over half the population now have private health insurance, and there is a thriving private health industry, which includes world-class hospitals and clinics. But for those who are unable to pay, medical care is getting worse and treatment can increasingly depend on getting help from a local charity hospital. The situation is worst of all for those living in *villas* and in poorer outlying provinces. Their survival rates from contagious diseases are lower, and poor sanitation and lack of clean water reduce their life expectancy considerably.

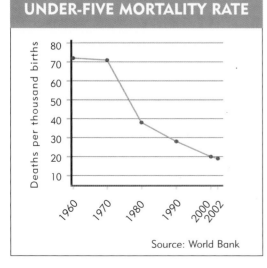

UNDER-FIVE MORTALITY RATE

Deaths per thousand births (80, 70, 60, 50, 40, 30, 20, 10) — years 1960, 1970, 1980, 1990, 2000, 2002

Source: World Bank

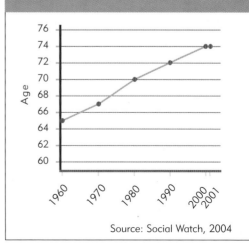

LIFE EXPECTANCY AT BIRTH

Age (76, 74, 72, 70, 68, 66, 64, 62, 60) — years 1960, 1970, 1980, 1990, 2000, 2001

Source: Social Watch, 2004

The Jesuit church of La Compañía in Córdoba, which was built in 1650.

RELIGION

Jesuit missionaries first brought Catholicism to the people of the north-east in the sixteenth century, and today nearly 90 per cent of Argentines are Roman Catholic. In 1989, the elected president, Carlos Menem, had to become a Catholic before taking office. Church weddings are still the usual way to get married – although a civil ceremony is also required – and the religious devotion of many can be seen in the celebration of Saints' days and the annual pilgrimage of thousands to the shrine of the Virgin of Luján. It is also common, for example, to see bus passengers crossing themselves whenever the bus passes a church.

However, the Catholic Church is far less influential than it is in other Latin American countries, and only 20 per cent of Argentine Catholics go to church regularly. Schools have been state run since the nineteenth century and many laws that were influenced by religion, such as the strict divorce laws, have

CASE STUDY
THE ARMENIAN CULTURAL CENTRES

Armenian Christians belong to one of Argentina's smaller religious groups. Proud of their Armenian heritage, they have built cultural centres across Argentina. In Córdoba, the Centro Armenio has close links with Córdoba's three Armenian churches, and also has an Armenian library and two sports clubs. Exchange visits to modern Armenia are organised, and the Centre also runs Armenian language and dance classes. There are two other centres in the country, the largest being in Buenos Aires.

Although their religion and Armenian origins are important to them, Armenian Christians do not forget that they are Argentines and must absorb Argentine customs too. Perhaps that is why one of the best-known tango (see page 39) schools in Argentina is in the cellar of the Buenos Aires Centro Armenio!

An Armenian wedding in Buenos Aires.

been removed. More importantly, immigration has introduced large religious minorities. South America's largest mosque is in Buenos Aires and there are estimated to be 800,000 Muslims in the country. Córdoba and five other cities across Argentina have synagogues; Buenos Aires has 16. These different religious groups generally live harmoniously with each other, although in 1994 the Buenos Aires Jewish community centre was bombed. The culprits are still to be found.

Argentina is unique in Latin America: religion is present but not dominant and belief is very much a private, personal affair, often linked to the customs and culture of the immigrant's home countries.

RELIGIOUS GROUPS

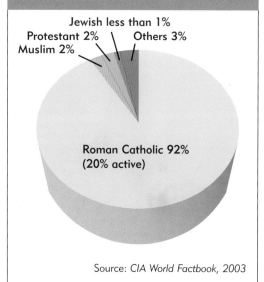

Jewish less than 1%
Protestant 2%   Others 3%
Muslim 2%

Roman Catholic 92%
(20% active)

Source: *CIA World Factbook, 2003*

CASE STUDY
SHRINES TO THE DIFUNTA CORREA

Travellers often come across roadside shrines to the Difunta Correa. People who believe in her powers say that while she was wandering in the desert near San Juan with her newborn baby, the Difunta died of thirst. Miraculously, her baby survived: mule drivers found the Difunta's withered body with the baby alive, still suckling at her breast. Since then, thousands of miracles have been connected to the Difunta. She is not a saint, but a 'soul' who is said to perform miracles.

Many Argentines ask for her help when they want a house, a car, a child, or a medical cure, for example. They make a pilgrimage to a shrine and they leave gifts. These gifts might be miniature models of houses and cars, family photos, candles, and water bottles to quench the Difunta's thirst.

Travellers asking for strength and protection at Vallecito, the most important shrine to the Difunta Correa, in San Juan province.

The Difunta is thought to protect travellers. Roads across the country are dotted with shrines, often with car parts attached to them as offerings for safe journeys.

The Catholic Church is unhappy with the shrines, believing them to be superstitious. However, up to 200,000 pilgrims visit the main shrine near San Juan at Easter and Christmas.

Family Life

The family is a very strong institution in Argentina and families with three or more children are common. Spending quality time together is very important, and most families have a daily evening meal together. Family birthdays are a major occasion, especially a daughter's fifteenth fiesta, or coming-of-age party. The second Sunday in August is *Día del Niño* or Children's Day – a big celebration with parties and presents.

Social security benefits encourage large families. Argentine families can get maternity benefit, marriage grants, a prenatal allowance, birth and adoption grants, child benefit and a school allowance. At 17.47 births per thousand people in 2003, the birth rate is higher than in Chile and Uruguay. However this disguises a recent trend towards smaller families. In the six years from 1998 to 2004, average family size fell from 2.7 to 2.2 children, and this pattern seems likely to continue.

Just as family size is falling, divorce rates are growing: 3.4 per cent of marriages now end in divorce, and nearly 6 per cent end in formal separation.

ABOVE: Argentine families are very close. Meals are an important time for families to come together.

BELOW: Shopping in the upmarket mall at Galerias Pacifico, central Buenos Aires.

FEMALE LABOUR FORCE (% OF TOTAL)

Year	Value
1965	23
1975	26
1985	28
1995	31
2000	33
2001	34

Source: Social Watch, 2004

THE ROLE OF WOMEN

Being a wife and a mother is central to traditional Argentine family values. Although men are the traditional breadwinners, since the early 1990s more married women have started to go out to work. Since 1980, the number of women in the workforce has increased by almost a third to 34 per cent.

Argentina is a very male-dominated society and the work done by many women reflects this. Around one in five work as maids, earning about 400 pesos a month. They live in the home of their employers, returning to their own family at the weekend.

The number of careers open to women has grown recently, encouraging educated women to get involved in a professional or commercial career. Teaching has always been a popular option, and the arrival of international companies in the 1990s has created new opportunities in media, law and management. These companies have less traditional male-based views of women than many Argentine firms.

LEISURE

Most leisure time is at the weekends, with Sunday being a day for all the family. Visiting friends, going dancing, to restaurants or to the cinema take place late at night, often after 10.00pm. January is the summer month when many families go on holiday. Many *porteños* go to the beach – to Pinamar in Argentina or to Punta del Este in Uruguay.

FOOTBALL

In Argentina football is not just a sport: it is a passion. It is played everywhere, in private sporting clubs, public neighbourhood parks and on any piece of unused land. Buenos Aires has half of the country's first division teams, including the two most famous: Boca Juniors and Río de la Plata. Many players begin their careers in Argentina, and then go on to play for European clubs. Football is also hugely popular on TV. Cable TV channels show football from all over the world, and fans can keep up with Argentine players in the Spanish, German, Italian and English leagues. Argentina's national side is one of the world's leading teams, having twice won the FIFA World Cup.

Football is a national passion. The fans of Boca Juniors show their colours.

CASE STUDY
WORLD CUP SUCCESS

Argentina has won the World Cup twice, in 1978 (when it also hosted the tournament) and in 1986. It also reached the final in 1930 and 1990.

For Argentines, World Cup success shows national achievement and gains international recognition. In a country where corruption is thought to be widespread, and where politics and economics have repeatedly failed, World Cup victory is seen by many as an opportunity for Argentina to show itself at its best. Victories in World Cup matches are met with instant celebrations on the streets. In 1998, when Argentina defeated England, traffic halted in the streets and people danced on the roofs of buses.

Diego Maradona is the country's most-adored footballer. Capped 91 times, he led Argentina to victory in 1986 and was voted the best player of the tournament. Despite later suspensions for drug-taking he remains a national icon of Argentina.

A couple learn to dance the tango at a class in Buenos Aires.

CINEMA ATTENDANCE (ANNUAL CINEMA VISITS PER 1,000 PEOPLE)

Argentina	838 per 1,000 people
Brazil	439 per 1,000 people
Chile	434 per 1,000 people
Bolivia	166 per 1,000 people

Source: UNESCO Institute for Statistics

DANCING

Argentina is the home of a dance called the tango. The tango demands skill and concentration, and it is taken very seriously. After a lull in the past, it has recently become very popular again and clubs have grown up across the country.

Argentines love all types of dancing, not just the tango. The milonga and the zamba are two other traditional dances, found most usually in the countryside. Club dancing late into the night is popular with teenagers. One difference with European clubbing is that there is far less emphasis on drinking alcohol: dancing is the main event.

EATING OUT

Eating out is very popular. Families eat out regularly and restaurants can be noisy places until late at night. The most traditional restaurants are beef restaurants called either *asados* or *parrillas*, depending on whether the meat is barbecued or grilled. The dishes are largely various cuts of beef served with a salad. Many are all inclusive, allowing you to eat all you can for a set price.

As a result of the large numbers of Italian immigrants, pizzerias and heladerías (ice-cream parlours) are found all over the country.

American fast-food chains are spreading across the country, including the development of fast-food courts in shopping malls. Some Argentines are concerned that this trend is beginning to have an effect on the country's eating habits and the health of young people.

TELEVISION SETS (PER 1,000 PEOPLE)

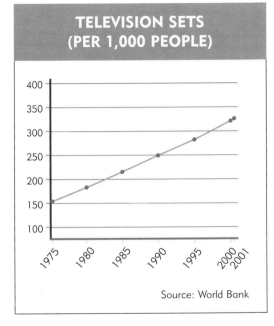

Source: World Bank

Pavement pizzerias and bars are popular throughout Argentina.

THE ECONOMY

Oxen haul a cart-load of tobacco leaves during the harvest in San Vicente.

AGRICULTURE

Cattle ranching and grain farming for cattle feed are the basis of Argentina's agricultural economy. Nearly 10 per cent of all land is used for growing crops, and 48 per cent for cattle pasture. The meat-processing industry has an estimated annual production valued at US$10 billion. It processes 12 million animals annually, of which 10.4 million are cattle. Argentina is the world's seventh-largest producer of dairy products and third-largest producer of powdered milk.

Farms cover huge areas – 4,000 hectares is considered small. In the past, farms were all family owned, but today some are run by cooperatives.

Because the country encompasses such a variety of climates and vegetation types, it is able to grow almost all the food it needs. The northern subtropical region around San Miguel de Tucumán produces cotton, sugar cane, tobacco, citrus and other fruits – Argentina is the world's leading exporter of lemon juice, fresh lemons, pears and apples. It also grows bananas, tea, some grains and oilseeds, as well as yerba mate, a herbal tea very popular in Argentina. The west, around Mendoza is home to the wine industry. Even in the cooler and drier south, in Chubut and Santa Cruz provinces, farmers graze sheep and angora goats for their fine wool. Berries, apples and pears are also produced there.

AGRICULTURE

- Wheat and maize
- Mixed farming
- Sugar
- Cattle
- Sheep
- Wooded grassland
- Wine

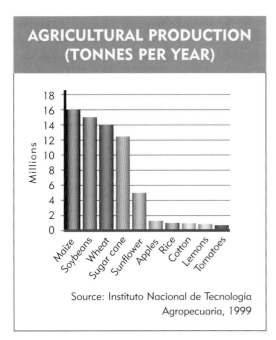

AGRICULTURAL PRODUCTION (TONNES PER YEAR)

Source: Instituto Nacional de Tecnología Agropecuaria, 1999

Loading trucks from the grain silos at harvest time, San Antonio de Areco.

However, it is the central Pampas region that is the largest agricultural producer. In addition to livestock farming, maize, wheat, sorghum, soybeans, flax, sunflowers, peanuts, apples, pears and citrus fruits are grown here, as well as most of the country's potatoes, flowers and non-tropical vegetables.

Although it is a key part of the Argentine identity, agriculture accounts directly for only 5 per cent of the country's GDP. Related industries, such as processing, transport and services increase this to 30 per cent. In the 1980s, food exports accounted for 80 per cent of export earnings. The economic changes of the 1990s saw this decline to below 60 per cent by 2000, and this was accompanied by a reduction in the workforce.

CASE STUDY
COMPETING IN WORLD MARKETS

Argentina produces much more than its home market requires and needs to export its large surplus. However, it has found itself increasingly excluded from traditional northern hemisphere markets. Trade blocs, such as the European Union and the North American Free Trade Association, make it hard for non-members like Argentina to trade with them. Tariff and non-tariff barriers, such as subsidies to European and US farmers, have hit Argentina's agricultural exports hard.

One response has been to diversify and find new markets. A new product is soybeans. From being practically unknown in Argentina a few years ago, soybean oil and flour now represent 40 per cent of the country's agrifood exports. Wine is a traditional product that is being marketed in a much more professional way towards northern hemisphere customers. Exports of quality wines rose 42 per cent between 1997 and 1998. Devaluation has given a further boost to sales overseas. Much (European) money has been invested in the industry, to set up cooperative groups and introduce new techniques and better grapes.

Niche export markets are also being explored. Traditionally, Argentine farming does not rely heavily on agrochemicals, and this is making it possible to produce organic food for the northern hemisphere. In March 2003, Argentina began exporting snails to Spain. There are 1,000 snail producers in the province of Córdoba alone.

Many genetically modified (GM) crops are grown in Argentina. Approximately 90 per cent of soybean, 17 per cent of maize and 10 per cent of cotton production is GM.

INDUSTRIAL DEVELOPMENT IN ARGENTINA

Industries processing agricultural products, such as meat-packing, cigarette manufacture and dairy production, are all significant today. Much of this industry is based in the provinces. In the north, for example, industries process sugar, paper, citrus fruits, leather, rice and tobacco. In Entre Ríos there are poultry – and citrus fruit – processing plants, dairies and cold storage plants. In the western Pampas and Cuyo the main products are wine, fruit and vegetable preserves and sunflower oil. Further south, in Río Negro province, there are factories making fruit and vegetable preserves and producing cider and wines, while Mar del Plata, on the coast, has fish-processing plants.

Light industries have grown up as a result of the economic priorities of 1940 to 1986, when the national aim was to reduce Argentina's dependence on imports. The centre – and the

A meat-packing plant in Rosario. Meat processing is Argentina's oldest manufacturing activity and has an estimated annual production valued at about US$10 billion, processing over 12 million head of livestock a year.

main market – for this light industrial development is the capital. The drive for self-sufficiency also led to the development of domestic energy sources. Petrochemical industries have been developed in Patagonia and the new northern oil fields in Salta.

More recently, attempts were made to promote industry and employment in the regions. In Patagonia this is done by subsidies for industry and lower tax rates for the population. Steel and aluminium smelting has been encouraged to use the energy resources found in the south and west.

MAIN AREAS OF EMPLOYMENT

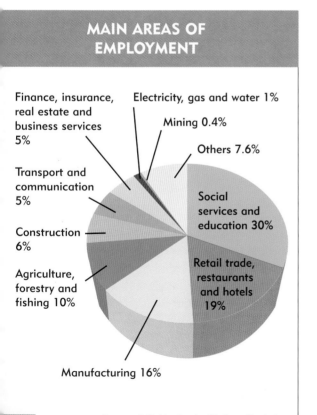

Finance, insurance, real estate and business services 5%

Electricity, gas and water 1%

Mining 0.4%

Others 7.6%

Transport and communication 5%

Construction 6%

Agriculture, forestry and fishing 10%

Social services and education 30%

Retail trade, restaurants and hotels 19%

Manufacturing 16%

Source: ILO, *Yearbook of Labour Statistics*

ECONOMIC STRUCTURE (% OF GDP), 2000

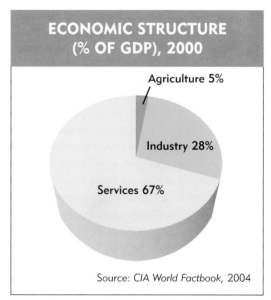

Agriculture 5%

Industry 28%

Services 67%

Source: *CIA World Factbook*, 2004

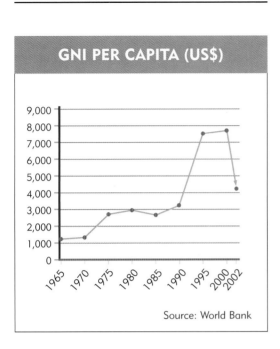

Source: World Bank

Córdoba, Argentina's second-largest city, has always been a major industrial centre with important flour, milk, oil and mechanical industries. It is also a producer of agricultural machinery. Córdoba is the centre of car production, much of which is exported to Mercosur members (see case study below), and a small aircraft industry, which was started after World War II by German manufacturers.

Assembling cars at the modern Renault plant in Córdoba.

CASE STUDY
MERCOSUR

During the 1990s, the world formed into large trading blocs, including NAFTA in North America and the EU in Europe. In South America, Mercosur was set up in 1995 by Argentina, Brazil, Paraguay and Uruguay with Chile as an associate member, in an effort to counter the threats of these large groups.

The aim of these countries is to encourage trade amongst themselves and to present a more united front to the trade barriers of the other world trade blocs.

Trade between members rose dramatically from US$4 billion in 1991 to over US$23 billion in 1998. More than 90 per cent of internal Mercosur trade is duty-free, while most goods imported from non-Mercosur countries are taxed. With a population of 220 million, the 2002 total output from the four Mercosur countries was US$561 billion. Trade talks with both NAFTA and the EU are underway to reduce trading barriers between each other's goods.

However members still act often in their own interests and against the aims of Mercosur. Brazil, Chile and Argentina have all discussed individual agreements with NAFTA and the EU.

THE NEW ECONOMY OF THE 1990s

In the 1980s Argentina, like many other South American countries, came out of military dictatorship and went into a time of massive inflation. In 1989, inflation hit 3,000 per cent and the peso was worthless. Unemployment grew rapidly and the rate of poverty in the country climbed to over 40 per cent of the population. Food riots broke out.

In 1988 Carlos Menem was elected President of Argentina. The government promised that savings and investments in pesos could be changed for US dollars at a rate of US$1 to 1 peso. This was called dollar convertibility and it was to be financed by selling state-owned businesses and encouraging foreign companies to set up in Argentina. The government privatised the railways, airlines, gas, electricity, water and postal services, and invited foreign companies to invest.

People were happy to work hard, spend and save knowing the peso was as good as the US dollar. Investors were also happy to buy and sell in Argentina again.

These policies revived the economy, ending hyperinflation and bringing a new prosperity to the country. Between 1995 and 1998, Argentina's economic growth was the highest in Latin America. Industrial production increased and there was a boom in consumer spending. With the economy doing so well,

EXPORTS AND IMPORTS

EXPORTS
1992 US$12 billion
1999 US$25 billion

IMPORTS
1992 US$15 billion
1999 US$25 billion

Source: *CIA World Factbook*, 2004

the Government could spend more in the poorer provinces to provide work. European companies rushed in to invest, largely in the utilities, banking and retailing.

The Argentine economy was seen by the International Monetary Fund (IMF) as a model for many other developing world economies. For the first time since 1900, the country's vast potential seemed to be being realised.

THE ECONOMIC COLLAPSE OF 2001–02

The Menem reforms brought serious consequences for the country. Dollar convertibility meant Argentina had less control over its economy than its Mercosur neighbours had over theirs. When Brazil devalued its currency in the late 1990s, goods produced in Argentina began to seem expensive by comparison. With costs cheaper

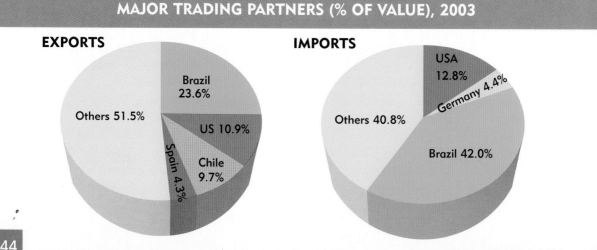

MAJOR TRADING PARTNERS (% OF VALUE), 2003

EXPORTS

Brazil 23.6%
Others 51.5%
US 10.9%
Spain 4.3%
Chile 9.7%

IMPORTS

USA 12.8%
Germany 4.4%
Others 40.8%
Brazil 42.0%

Source: *CIA World Factbook*, 2004

A barter market in the San Telmo neighbourhood of Buenos Aires in 2002.

in Brazil, overseas owners closed down Argentine factories, and unemployment rose.

As the economy slowed down, government spending on social welfare, schools and health was cut. The government borrowed a great deal of money from overseas banks and the IMF. Borrowing increased in other ways too. Companies had been borrowing to help them expand, and consumers were buying on credit. When the boom ended, these loans could not be repaid and Argentina went deeper into recession.

Many provinces began to print their own money to pay pensions, benefits and salaries. With less to spend, people bought less. In 2002 supermarket sales were 24 per cent less than in 2001. Unemployment rose to 25 per cent. In the cities, 44 per cent of people were officially classified as poor, with an income of less than 120 pesos a month. People resorted to bartering for essentials. Foreign banks and companies moved their deposits outside the country.

Finally, in January 2002, dollar convertibility was ended and the peso was devalued. The middle classes, who had saved at the promised dollar convertibility rate of 1US$ to 1 peso, now saw their savings disappear as bank accounts were blocked and the peso fell to less than US30 cents.

Public demonstrations (characterised by *cacerolazos*, or people banging cooking pots) led by the middle classes attacked government policies and the role of foreign banks and companies in the collapse. A succession of governments fell. Eventually new agreements were signed with the IMF, allowing for personal savings to be released, and a recovery began to take place.

Cacerolazos (pot-bangers) protest during the economic collapse.

THE COLLAPSE IN FIGURES

PRODUCTION	1999	2000	2001
Cigarettes (thousands of packs of 20)	1,996,000	1,843,000	739,000
Passenger motor vehicles	225,000	239,000	170,000
Refrigerators	354,000	325,000	246,000
Construction cement (million tonnes)	7,187	6,114	5,545

Source: Instituto Nacional de Estadística y Censos

Hiking in the Cerro Fitzroy range of the Parque Nacional los Glaciares, Patagonia

TOURISM

Argentina has much to offer tourists: glaciers and subtropical rainforests; mountains and lakes; high arid deserts and the attractions of Buenos Aires. All types of tourism are catered for. People can go city sightseeing in the capital, riding on an estancia, skiing in the Andes, whale-watching in the Valdes Peninsula and see the spectacular scenery of the southern glaciers and the Iguazú Falls in the north-east. Until recently, Argentina has been slow to market its attractions but since devaluation, this has changed and tourism is one of the country's fastest growing sectors and a major foreign currency earner.

The devaluation (see page 44–45) has had major effects on tourism. With the collapse of the peso, Argentina became much cheaper for foreigners. The Ministry of Tourism believes that the number of foreigners entering Argentina will increase from 3 million in 2003 to 10 million by 2010. From December 2002 to April 2003, 19 per cent of foreign tourists came from Europe, 12 per cent from the USA and Canada, and 13 per cent from the rest of the world. The remainder came from neighbouring Mercosur countries and Chile. These foreign tourists spend over US$2.8 billion each year in the country. Unable to travel abroad because of their weak currency, more Argentines choose to take their holidays in Argentina.

TRANSPORT LINKS

A network of air routes connects all Argentina's main centres. However, not all routes make money and airline bankruptcies are common. Aerolíneas Argentinas has an extensive international network, but since the 2002 economic collapse, many international airlines have closed down direct flights.

TRANSPORT

BOLIVIA
PARAGUAY
N

San Salvador de Jujuy
Salta
San Miguel de Tucumán
Santiago del Estero

BRAZIL

San Juan
Córdoba
Santa Fé
URUGUAY

Mendoza
Rosario
Buenos Aires

San Antonio de Areco
La Plata

Mar del Plata

Bahía Blanca

San Carlos de Bariloche

PACIFIC OCEAN

Comodoro Rivadavia

—— Main road
······ Railway
✈ International airport
⚓ Port

0   500km
0   300 miles

Santa Cruz

Falkland Islands (UK)

Tierra del Fuego

Ushuaia

TELECOMMUNICATIONS DATA (PER 1,000 PEOPLE)	
Mainline Phones	219
Mobile Phones	178
Internet Users	112

Source: World Bank

Passengers boarding a regional flight at Córdoba airport.

The railways were one of the first industries to be privatised in the 1990s and, outside the capital, most were soon closed down and replaced by long-distance coach routes. For most Argentines, modern, comfortable coaches are now the main form of transport within the country. Journeys are long but cheap: Buenos Aires to Córdoba takes 10 hours but costs less than US$30; Iguazú to the capital takes 21 hours and costs US$40.

There are 11,000km of navigable rivers, mostly in the network of the de la Plata, Paraguay, Uruguay and Paraná river systems. This carries most Mercosur bulk freight, and vessels can sail 3,500km inland through Uruguay, Paraguay, Brazil, and Bolivia. A fast, modern catamaran service carries passengers and cars between Buenos Aires and Uruguay.

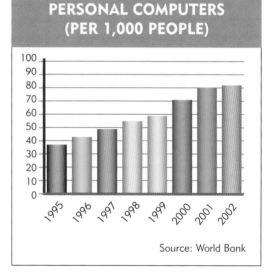

PERSONAL COMPUTERS (PER 1,000 PEOPLE)

Source: World Bank

CASE STUDY
ARGENTINA AND THE INTERNET

In 1990, Argentina lagged far behind in new communications technology. It took 1,400 days to have a telephone connected; in 2001 it took just 10 days. Big advances have since been made in new technology, and today Argentina is the country with the highest number of domestic PCs in the Spanish-speaking world. With 3.88 million Internet users, only Brazil makes more use of the Web in South America. Internet usage has grown 64 per cent since 2000 and the Government has introduced schemes aimed at making the Internet available across the vast expanses of the country.

However, Argentina faces problems common to many other poorer countries. The highest growth in Internet usage is in the cities, not in the vast, sparsely populated areas that could benefit most from it. Away from the cities, obstacles are basic. Some years ago, the Argentine Government sent computers to schools in the very poor northern province of Jujuy – but the schools had no electricity. A survey in January 2001, showed that, of those without a computer, 56 per cent could not afford one.

THE ENVIRONMENT

Capybaras, the world's largest rodents, are found in the swamp lands of the north-east.

The changes to Argentina's economy during the 1990s put new pressures on the environment. From north to south, the country now faces huge environmental issues: Argentina is one of South America's largest polluters, and human development is having a big impact on the country's many different ecological habitats.

Argentina's environmental problems are those of an industrialising economy: soil degradation, desertification, and air and water pollution. Recent governments have given commitments to improve the situation, but economic and political problems make success uncertain.

MESOPOTAMIA

Meaning 'between the rivers', the area known as Mesopotamia stretches north between the Paraná and Uruguay rivers, from the Pampas plains to Iguazú. Much of the region is made up of swampy lowland forests and upland savannahs. Flooding is a regular event due to

CASE STUDY
THE FLOODS OF 1998

The Paraná is the most important tributary of the Río de la Plata, and its basin covers 1.5 million km². In April 1998, the Paraná River basin flooded as a result of strong storms and exceptional rainfall caused by El Niño. The flooding affected a vast area, including the provinces of Corrientes, Misiones, Entre Ríos, Santa Fé, Chaco and Formosa. More than 32,000 people were evacuated and 100,000 people in Chaco were isolated by the

floodwaters. Corrientes was the hardest hit. The province contains one of the largest inland wetlands in the world, the Esteros del Iberá. In many places rivers burst their banks, causing serious damage to settlements and farming, and destroying roads.

The flooding caused serious damage to crops and livestock. The rice crop was almost completely destroyed and total agricultural losses exceeded US$300 million. The people most affected were the poorest, who lived in the most flood-prone areas, and many lost their entire harvest. It took months for the water to drain away.

LEFT: A victim of the 1998 El Niño flooding being rescued by neighbours north of Santa Fé.

CASE STUDY
DEFORESTATION IN SAN PEDRO

high annual rainfall. A combination of haphazard human development and the effects of global warming are producing significant environmental problems. Human settlements are encroaching on the subtropical forests of the north and upsetting the ecology of the rivers. In 1996 the World Bank reported that road construction, followed by poorly planned urban expansion, and effluent from the meat-packing industry were the major factors causing environmental damage. It also found that many ecosystems and human activities depended on the regular floods. A policy of 'living with floods' was adopted. Unfortunately, a combination of increased rainfall due to global warming, and a lack of effective government strategy, have meant that recent years have seen ever bigger floods. In 1998 (see case study on page 48), 2001 (about 3.5 million hectares under water) and 2003 (100,000 homeless in Santa Fé) massive flooding has revealed just how disastrous flooding is to both the local population and the natural ecology.

San Pedro is a small north-eastern town in Misiones. It is in one of the main areas where the araucaria tree grows. More usually called the monkey puzzle tree, it is valued for the quality of its timber. Originally, the tree grew widely across the northern hemisphere but now it is only found in temperate regions of South America and Australia.

In San Pedro, the trees are being felled not just for their timber. As the town expands and reaches the edge of the forest, the araucarias are cut down to make room for houses. As the forest disappears, so do its rare breeds of birds and animals. One example is the vinaceous-breasted parrot. This is an endangered species, found only in the subtropical forests of Brazil and northern Argentina. The loss of its natural habitat – the araucaria tree – is reducing its numbers to a dangerously low level.

BELOW: The outskirts of San Pedro showing deforestation. Shacks have been built where araucaria trees have been felled.

THE PAMPAS STEPPE

The Pampas is one of the few remaining regions where semi-arid Pampas grasses are still found. Although it is an area of high biodiversity, most natural vegetation has been replaced by cultivated crops.

Animals still found in the wild include the pampa deer, puma and pampa fox. The Pampas is also home to the rhea and various bird species such as the caracara, kite and great kiskadee.

Increasing agricultural land use is a major threat to the ecological balance. Agriculture reduces the natural vegetation, and intensive irrigation (needed to supply crops and animals with water) drains the area's natural wetlands. A further threat is likely to come from the genetically modified crops currently being planted. Being resistant to disease, they may outgrow existing plant species and thus reduce the food available for insects and other animals.

Much of Argentina's industrial activity takes place on the Pampas. This includes mining, smelting and oil extraction and refining. These generate a considerable amount of pollution both in their immediate vicinity

ABOVE: A wind-driven water pump on the Pampas.

BELOW: Rheas – large flightless birds – wild on the Pampas.

Waste disposal is well managed in Buenos Aires, and daily collections remove household rubbish from the streets. But it is common for much of the rubbish to be taken before the waste-disposal trucks arrive. An army of poor people – 40,000 according to a recent government report – travels the streets looking for rubbish to sell for recycling. These so-called *cartoneros* are often complete families from the local *villa*. Unemployment means they have no regular income. They are paid very little for their work: on a good night, the family can salvage 200kg of waste and make 10 or 12 pesos. For many it is their only income – and it helps to recycle the city's waste.

Cartoneros collecting rubbish for recycling on a Buenos Aires street.

and downstream in other communities. Refineries in particular have caused pollution of groundwater and underground aquifers with chemicals such as mercury, lead and other toxins.

Attempts to create conservation areas have met with only limited success. For example, a project to create a protected reserve in San Luis province has not been completed and roads are still being built across areas vital for its conservation. Pampa deer numbers are continuing to fall due to poaching.

POLLUTION IN BUENOS AIRES

Each day, 12 million workers commute into and around the capital. The city's 8 million cars and large fleet of buses account for 60 per cent of the total number of automobiles in Argentina and create serious health problems for the city.

Industry adds to the pollution. In 1997, industries produced 15.1 million metric tons of carbon – 43 per cent of Argentina's carbon emissions – mostly in the capital. Air pollution has always been a problem in Buenos Aires. In 2000, the Buenos Aires government introduced incentives for vehicles to switch from petrol to cleaner fuels, such as LPG (liquefied petroleum gas).

Water pollution is another city problem. Industrial and domestic waste seeps illegally into rivers and contaminates water supplies. As a result, bottled drinking water is a major industry. Heavy rainfall overloads the outdated drainage system and flooding is becoming more and more common. Aguas Argentinas, the privatised water company, is renewing much of the city's old water and sewage systems, upgrading them to meet the demands of a larger population and to cope with intense storms.

THE PATAGONIAN STEPPE

Patagonia's natural vegetation includes grassland, scrub forest, deciduous thicket and wetlands. It is home to many large mammals; including guanacos (a type of llama), and sea lions that breed along the coastline, as well as rodents such as guinea pigs and mice. There are several specialised species, including burrowing owls, and nocturnal creatures, such as the Patagonian opossum.

There are many national parks and protected reserves but, although few people live in Patagonia, there are serious man-made threats to the fragile environment. Coal, natural gas and oil are extracted, causing pollution and upsetting the local ecology. Desertification occurs due to overgrazing by sheep and other animals introduced by settlers, such as horses, cattle and rabbits.

This damages the natural plant cover and causes soil erosion. Soil erosion also takes place because of shrub-clearing along rivers to increase farming land. Some animals, such as guanacos, are hunted for their furs. Others, including foxes and pumas, are hunted by farmers as pests.

THE ANTARCTIC TERRITORIES

Argentina's Antarctic territorial claims include settlements in the South Shetlands and the Antarctic peninsula itself. In the Antarctic, the land is covered by snow all year round. Even outside the ice, little grows except for mosses, lichens and algae. Summer temperatures rarely rise much above freezing, while in winter they can fall to –25°C. Wildlife depends on the sea. Seals share seafood with an estimated 350 million birds, half of which are penguins.

CASE STUDY
THE VALDES PENINSULA AND ECO-TOURISM

The Valdes Peninsula is one of the main centres of marine life in Argentina, and is a UNESCO world heritage site. Magellan penguins have rookeries along the coastline, and sea lions breed on the beaches in spring, attracting killer whales that hunt the seal pups. Southern right whales come to raise their young in one of the world's largest whale mating grounds. Between 2,000 and 3,000 of the 6,000 whales that populate the world's oceans come to breed here.

Tourism is growing but is well regulated. Seabirds on the small Isla de los Pajores can only be viewed by telescope from the peninsula, and whale-watchers must follow tight rules designed to protect the whales. Tightly enforced regulations place the entire beach area out of bounds. The only hotel is a small converted lighthouse, and most visitors stay in nearby Puerto Madryn and travel around the reserve in small groups with official rangers.

A sea lion colony on the Valdes Peninsula during the breeding season.

Argentina regards the Falkland Islands as part of its territory, and refers to them as Las Malvinas. Originally settled by the French and Spanish, the islands became Argentine in 1820. In 1833 they came under British rule, but Argentina has claimed them ever since.

The settlement of Pebble Station on the Falkland Islands.

In 1982, an Argentine military occupation was ended by a British task force. The consequences for Argentina were considerable, as defeat brought an end to the military dictatorship that had controlled the country since 1976. It was not until 2000 that regular contact between Argentina and the islands was re-established.

The ecosystem is very vulnerable, and tourism and private summer yachting are growing problems. Both can produce pollution and disruption to natural habitats. Between 1992 and 2003, annual tourist numbers doubled from 6,500 to 13,000.

Additional threats come from global problems. A hole in the ozone layer, caused by CFC (chloroflurocarbon) pollution in the atmosphere was first noticed in 1984. The hole exposes the region to increased solar radiation. Global warming also threatens the Antarctic ice sheet. The melting of the ice could seriously affect the plant and wildlife of Argentina and beyond.

Whale-watching off the Valdes Peninsula is popular with eco-tourists but is tightly controlled to protect the sealife.

LOOKING AHEAD

Florida, the main shopping street in downtown Buenos Aires.

ECONOMIC POTENTIAL

Argentina had a difficult start to the twenty-first century. Economic collapse brought long-term unemployment and lost savings. The peso now buys much less than it did in 2001, and massive loans still need to be repaid.

CASE STUDY
THE MILITARY DICTATORSHIP

In 1976, after a period of violence and terrorism, a group of military leaders – known as the Junta – seized power. Political parties were made illegal and opponents were arrested. As many as 30,000 people disappeared, never to be heard of again.

Economic failure and defeat in the Falklands War eventually brought down the Junta and democracy returned. Today the 'Mothers of the Disappeared' demonstrate each week to remind Argentines of this period and to seek justice for the death of their children.

The regular Thursday afternoon demonstration by the Mothers of the Disappeared outside the Presidential Palace.

A large container ship berthed at Ushuaia's modern docks in Tierra del Fuego. The south of Argentina receives many incentives to encourage industrial development.

Yet the country is recovering. It has huge natural resources, which are being exported thanks to the weaker peso making them cheaper. The IMF (International Monetary Fund) has not always helped Argentina in the past by encouraging privatisation and borrowing, but it is now giving the country more time to repay the loans. Argentina is beginning to live on what it has, not what it can borrow.

The signs of recovery are clear: inflation fell from 30 per cent in 2003 to 3 per cent in 2004. Energy consumption has risen so much it is causing shortages and power cuts. In 2004, GDP grew by 7 per cent a year. Many young skilled Argentines who left in 2001 and 2002 are returning. Rising incomes mean that more taxes are being paid, which helps to finance the welfare system.

Argentina has not made the best use of its real potential during the last 100 years. Perhaps the present recovery will allow it to do so.

POLITICAL PROBLEMS

Argentina has had as many political problems as it has had economic crises. Governments have allied themselves either with the poor or the landowning elites, while politicians who tried to appeal to the middle classes have tended to be weak and ineffective. Since 1914 the military have siezed power twice. Many Argentines distrust their politicians. There is a widespread belief that politicians are corrupt.

Carlos Menem, the president behind the reforms of the 1990s was charged with corruption, and this led to disillusionment, strikes, demonstrations and riots. It also deflected attention away from economic growth. A successful future will need a political system that Argentines trust.

THE CHALLENGE OF THE FUTURE

Argentina is already recovering from the economic collapse of 2002, and the social upheaval it brought with it. In terms of its natural resources, Argentina is one of the world's richest nations. Argentines talk about *solidaridad* – social solidarity: people working together, helping each other and sharing responsibilities.

The chaos of 2002 made many Argentines believe that their government did not listen to them. All over the country, local communities set up their own assemblies – *asambleas barriales* – to talk and deal with the everyday issues that affected them. These assemblies are based on the *barrio*, or neighbourhood, and decisions are made by local people who attend meetings held in local squares or in schools. At first they met to find ways to cope

CASE STUDY
THE BRUKMAN OCCUPATION

In December 2001, the Brukman clothing factory was occupied by its workers. The owner had gone bankrupt and wanted to close the factory. Since then, the workers have paid the outstanding bills, attracted new clients and paid themselves steady wages. Most are women between the ages of 40 and 65, mainly from Argentina's impoverished northern provinces.

Attempts were made to evict them both by the police and by the old owner, who saw the

Brukman workers take cover during a tear gas attack by riot police.

factory in profit. After each attempt, factory machines were destroyed, making it difficult for the women to restart production. In October 2003, the Buenos Aires city government voted to allow the workers' occupation, as the factory had been declared bankrupt before it was occupied.

A road blockade by *piqueteros* in Misiones province.

with immediate problems: they set up exchange and barter markets, and discussed how economic change would affect them. Although some assemblies are no longer active, the surviving ones now see themselves as an alternative, more democratic, way of dealing with local needs. They are helping people to play an important part in their own future and in a new type of Argentine democracy.

Many groups in Argentine society still feel excluded and ignored, and they frequently resort to direct action. *Piqueteros* (pickets) – drawn from the unemployed, the *villa* populations and the provincial poor – blockade roads and make demands on the national government. They call for more jobs, better welfare provision and an end to what they claim is police brutality. Workers facing unemployment occupy their workplaces in an effort to stay in work and manage themselves. These conflicts, which often end in violence, reveal the cracks in society.

If Argentina is to achieve its potential, these groups will have to be integrated into society so that the economic opportunities opened up by devaluation and new patterns of trade can improve life for all Argentines. That is the challenge of the twenty-first century.

CASE STUDY
THE GAUDALUPE ASAMBLEA BARRIAL

The Gaudalupe neighbourhood assembly was set up in 2001 in a district of Santa Fé, an industrial port. It represents the local community and makes its views known through regular meetings. One of its main priorities is working with the neighbourhood to prevent youth crime and to support family values. After putting pressure on the provincial government, it received funding to build, open and help manage a new health centre with a doctor, a dentist, a laboratory and health education facilities. It also operates a local library and, with funding from the Ministry of Trade, runs training courses in business management and information technology. It supports a local radio station and has its own website.

Water is a key concern in Santa Fé. During the 2002 floods, the *asamblea* helped organise accommodation for homeless families. It is now campaigning against the multinational company that holds the water supply concession. It claims too little is being done to provide quality water at reasonable cost or to control flooding.

Recent increases in soybean exports have made Argentina the world's third-largest producer of the crop.

GLOSSARY

Arid A term used to describe an environment with an annual rainfall that is below 250–300mm.

Authoritarian A government demanding total obedience and refusing to allow people freedom to act as they wish.

Blue-nose warehou A fish that is found in the colder areas of the southern Atlantic Ocean.

Caranday palm A slow-growing palm with blue-grey fan shaped leaves and a brown fibrous trunk. It can reach a height of 4m.

Cooperative A business, such as a farm, that is owned by all the people who work in it.

Deforestation The clearance of trees, either for timber or for land.

Democracy A political system in which people choose the leaders they want to run the country by voting for them in elections.

Desertification The creation of deserts by changes in climate, or by human-aided processes such as overgrazing, destruction of forests and soil exhaustion by intensive cultivation.

Devaluation When the value of a currency falls compared with other countries' currencies.

Diversification Broadening an economy or business by adding new activities.

Dorado A large, aggressive freshwater fish that can weigh up to 25kg. It is called 'the tiger of the river'.

Ecosystem A system that represents the relationships within a community of living things and between this community and their non-living environment. An ecosystem can be as small as a pond or as large as the Earth.

Eco-tourism Tourism that is sensitive to its impact on environments and local populations.

El Niño A change in the Pacific Ocean currents that causes severe weather and, especially, increased rainfall.

Erosion The removal of soil and rock by natural forces (wind and rain) or people (deforestation).

GDP (Gross Domestic Product) The total value of a country's goods. Often quoted as per capita, i.e., the amount per person.

Global warming The increase in temperatures around the world, which many scientists believe is caused by an increase in pollution in the atmosphere.

GM Genetically modified crops grown from seeds that have been changed in some way to make them produce a bigger crop, or more resistant to disease.

GNI (Gross National Income) The monetary value of goods and services produced by a country plus any earnings from overseas in a single year. It used to be called Gross National Product (GNP).

Habitat The natural home of a living thing.

Hyperinflation When prices rise extremely rapidly and people cannot afford to buy even basic goods.

Immigration The movement of people into a country, city or other place, to live.

Indigenous People descended from the native, pre-European population.

Jesuit A member of the Roman Catholic Society of Jesus founded in 1534 and devoted to missionary and educational work.

Loess Fertile yellow soil coming from glacial meltwater.

Mercosur (Mecado Común del Cono Sur) A trading bloc consisting of the countries of what is called the Southern Cone – Argentina, Brazil, Paraguay, Uruguay and Chile.

Mestizo A Spanish word describing people of mixed indigenous and European race.

Monopoly A situation in which one company controls an industry and there is no competition.

Montane A mountainous area.

Moraine The rocky debris or till carried along and deposited by a glacier.

Multinational (corporation) A large business that has operations in a number of countries.

NAFTA North American Free Trade Association (USA, Canada and Mexico).

Nomadic A farming system in which livestock are taken to different locations in order to find fresh pastures.

Productivity The output achieved from a certain level of resource use, investment and effort.

Savannah A dryland ecosystem dominated by grassland with scattered trees and bushes.

Sedimentary rock Rock formed by the building up of deposits laid down by water, wind, or ice – for example, limestone, shale and sandstone.

Snout The front end of a glacier, representing the furthest advance of the ice at any one time.

Steppe Temperate grasslands. Arable and pastoral farming are carried out there.

Streamflow The quantity of water flowing in a river.

Tariff A tax on imports, intended to protect local products from cheap imports.

Tectonic The rock structures resulting from changes to the Earth's crust.

Temperate Usually refers to climates without great extremes of heat or cold.

Villas Shanty towns, originally called *villas de emergencia* (emergency settlements) for the poor.

Welfare state A country where the government provides help and support for everyone in need: the sick, the unemployed, the young and the old.

Yerba mate A tea-like drink, popular in Argentina and Uruguay, made from the dried leaves of the yerba plant.

FURTHER INFORMATION

BOOKS TO READ:

NON-FICTION:

Lonely Planet Guide: Argentina, Uruguay and Paraguay by Sandra Bao (Lonely Planet, 4th Edition 2002) Budget travel guide for travellers of all ages. Good background information sections.

Footprint Handbook: Argentina by Charlie Nurse (Footprint Handbooks, 2000) Very informative guide book. Well researched with good information boxes.

Insight Guides: Argentina (Insight Guides, 2002) Visually well produced.

Far Away and Long Ago, A History of My Early Life by W H Hudson (The Lyons Press, 1997) A classic memoir of boyhood in the Pampas of Argentina, especially strong on the descriptions of landscapes, birds and nature.

The Last Cowboys at the End of the World: The Story of the Gauchos of Patagonia by Nick Reding (Crown, 2001) The story of the last genuine gauchos.

Maradona by Lian Goodall (Warwick Publishing, 1999) A biography of Argentina's soccer hero.

WEBSITES:

GENERAL INFORMATION:

El Sur del Sur
http://www.surdelsur.com
Colourful and detailed site run by the Argentine Department of Culture.

Geographia
http://www.geographia.com/argentina/index.html
A clearly set out guide to Argentina and its regions.

The Economist
http://economist.com/countries/Argentina/index.cfm
Good up-to-date information from *The Economist* magazine and special reports on Argentina.

The CIA World Factbook
http://www.cia.gov/cia/publications/factbook/geos/ar.html
Maps and many, many facts from the CIA.

About Inc.
http://gosouthamerica.about.com/cs/argentina/
This webpage has links to sites on nearly all aspects of Argentine life. Specially designed for schools.

STATISTICS:

Latin Focus
http://www.latin-focus.com/
The Europa World Year Book Online
http://www.europaworld.com/entry/ar
These sites are very good for up-to-date information, clearly set out.

SOCIETY:

Citizenship and Immigration Canada
http://www.settlement.org/cp/english/argentina/
A broad survey of Argentine life by the Canadian citizenship and immigration office.

ENVIRONMENT:

Animals of Argentina
http://www.geocities.com/fotosaves/index_english.html
Very good visual site on animals and birds of Argentina.

Wild World
http://www.worldwildlife.org/wildworld/
WWF in collaboration with National Geographic. Detailed reports on each Argentinian eco-region.

INDEX

Numbers shown in **bold** refer to pages with maps, graphic illustrations or photographs.

A couple dance the tango, busking in Plaza Dorrego, Buenos Aires.

A high-speed catamaran ferry on the Río de la Plata.